The Unsettling Season_____

The Unsettling Season

Donald J. Shelby

UPPER
ROOM BOOKS
NASHVILLE

The Unsettling Season

Cover Design: Karen Horner/Jackson Design
Book Design: Jim Bateman
First Printing: September 1989 (7)
Library of Congress Catalog Card Number: 88-051469
ISBN: 0-8358-0596-4

Printed in the United States of America.

This is for Chuck Wiggins,
esteemed colleague
and cherished friend.

Acknowledgements_____

I cherish the Advents spent with God's people in the First United Methodist Church of Santa Monica. My secretary, Sandi Agnew, went many second miles in preparing the manuscript. Gerald and Elizabeth Jennings graciously opened to me their home in Pauma Valley as the place where I could write. In the love of my wife, Jean, and my daughters, Darla and Dana, the Advent trumpet sounds and readies me to meet the Messiah.

Contents

Introduction

In *Walking on Water* Madeleine L'Engle comments that "the Christian holiday which is easiest for us is Christmas, because it touches on what is familiar; and the story . . . is one we have always known." That, however, may be both bane and blessing, and it may explain why we let the folklore, customs, and frantic pace of this holy season obscure its essential truth for us. Overfamiliarity can dull the meaning and diminish our response to any experience or relationship in life. Is that why many persons approach Christmas with either wistful yearning or cynical disdain, hoping each year to see, as W. H. Auden put it, "the actual Vision" of Christmas, or having missed it so often no longer believing the "Vision" exists?

Because we need to see this vision and to appropriate for faith the truth that Christmas celebrates, the church long ago set aside a margin of time celebrating the event of Jesus' birth so that believers could center attention more closely upon its deepest meaning, be nurtured by it, and respond to it. They called it the season of *Advent* (a Latin word meaning "come to"), underscoring how in this event God came to the world, entered human history, and is still revealing the love that makes us whole and opens us to eternal life.

We need a season of Advent to interrupt and unsettle us, to give us pause, to make us ponder, and to challenge our intentions and priorities. We need this season because we can be creatures of habit and routine who take each other and our spiritual life for granted. We need this season because we are prone to reduce the mysterious in order to make it manageable and marketable. We need this season as a reminder that our encounter with God through Christ can forever change our life and our world.

Dare we spend the days of Advent with a sense of anticipation and wonder? Dare we set aside times for prayer and meditation in which we determine where the growing edges of life are for us, in which we reverence the greatness of God and open ourselves to the Spirit's leading? Dare we study the scriptures and listen for the word God may speak to us? Dare we prepare to meet the Messiah and then to follow him into the needs of human hearts and into experiences of reconciliation? Dare we take time to join a small face-to-face study or spiritual growth group where dialogue and reinforcement challenge and encourage us? The answer must be yes, for there is much that is waiting to happen in us and between us and in our world.

This book has been written as a resource for such reflection, dialogue, and expectant waiting. It can be used for individual study and meditation or in a group setting. Following an introductory chapter, there are additional chapters for each of the four weeks of Advent, moving to the Feast of the Nativity of Our Lord. The sixth chapter looks to Epiphany and its emphasis on showing Christ forth. Included with each chapter are selected passages of scripture for study and interpretation. To further prompt group discussion or individual reflection, questions and other suggesstions are offered.

There is no more fertile setting for spiritual growth and insight than in a small face-to-face group where, in the context of scriptural truth, people engage in dialogue and exploration, sharing their concerns and discoveries, voicing their questions and doubts, and opening themselves to new understandings and breakthroughs. A leader or facilitator can help guide the group and keep it focused. Other resources can be used as background information. Prayer at the beginning and close of each session will, of course, be an important part of each gathering. You will find a selection of prayers you may wish to use at the end of this book. Most groups will discover how the Holy Spirit prompts insights and connections that no framed question or printed resource can ever anticipate. Other moments will emerge that call for silence or celebration instead of conversation and discussion.

Indeed, Advent is not so much what we do (no matter how devoted or disciplined we are) but what God does for us in Jesus Christ. "And the Word became flesh and dwelt among us, full of grace and truth; we have beheld his glory, glory as of the only

Son from the Father. . . . And from his fulness have we all received, grace upon grace" (John 1:14, 16). So let us attend upon this mystery and celebrate how God comes into our world—and into your life and mine—in Jesus Christ with the whole-making power of love.

Chapter One _____

Watching and Waiting Expectantly

For still the vision awaits its time;
   it hastens to the end—it will not lie.
If it seems slow, wait for it;
   it will surely come, it will not delay.

                         —Habakkuk 2:3

Read: *Jeremiah 33:14-16; Habakkuk 1–2:4;*
 Mark 13:32-37.

I will never forget how an eighteen-month-old child named Jessica McClure, trapped in an abandoned well shaft in Midland, Texas, captured the nation's attention. During the almost fifty-nine-hour vigil kept with her and the scores of rescue workers who struggled so desperately to reach and save the helpless child, I learned again what watching and waiting feel like existentially. I ached for her parents as they peered into the black shaft that encased their baby, as they listened to her hum verses from a Winnie-the-Pooh song. I wanted to be there with the oil-field workers and other rescue and medical experts who struggled feverishly against death and time—who drilled and clawed their way to the child, overcoming one obstacle after another. Television cameras recorded faces on which were written anguish, concern, and determination. When the breakthrough moment finally came on that Friday night in October and a paramedic emerged with baby Jessica in his arms, the eyes of the nation filled with tears and voices let out a cry of gratitude to God.

Watching and waiting are a perennial part of life. Such intervals challenge us and reveal a great deal about the structure of our character, the strength of our love, and the depth of our faith. Various writers refer to such waiting and watching as "The Test" or

17

"The Ordeal" or "The Moment of Truth." To describe the act of waiting and watching, theologian Belden C. Lane uses the anthropological term *liminality*, which comes from the Latin for *threshold*. I think he is right, for to watch and wait is to stand on a threshold, poised betwixt and between. It is to exist in an interim status, to feel suspended between what has been and what will be, to confront and affirm new meanings that take us beyond cherished opinions and familiar points of reference. A sense of such threshold is sometimes experienced in the context of today's jet air travel when, within a matter of a few short hours, we are transferred from recognizable settings to unfamiliar locales, cultures, and time zones among strangers who speak a different language. While in the air we are poised between two worlds—straddling two thresholds!

Advent is such a liminality—a threshold, if you will—a season of passage and discovery, a time of waiting and watching. Advent celebrates the coming of God, the entrance of the Holy One into human history in the person of Jesus Christ. He *came* 2,000 years ago into the Greco-Roman world of Caesar Augustus and was born a child in Bethlehem of Judea. He also *comes* now into our world and meets us as Risen Lord where and when we least expect him. He *will come again* when God brings this world and human history to an end. Christ's coming always creates a threshold, for through him God opens new horizons, inaugurates a new age, and so unsettles us into greater becoming and deeper understanding that we experience a new life. In this new life we leave what once was and we venture forth to what is yet to be fulfilled.

This coming of God into the world and to the Hebrews as God's chosen people comprised a recurrent theme of the Hebrew prophets who stood in the long heritage of their community of faith. We cannot begin to make sense of the prophetic message without it, nor can we understand the dynamics of the covenantal relationship which the Hebrew people claimed with God, reaching back to the patriarch Abraham. The suggested references from the Old Testament at the end of this chapter are only a brief sampling, but they reveal how deeply such hope was cherished and what tremendous inspiration it generated in the people, especially when their nation was finally destroyed and most of the people were taken away into exile.

God's divine intervention had blessed and judged the Hebrew people in the past, had made covenant with them and given them the Law, and had raised up King David and his successors on the throne as "anointed ones" to guarantee the peace and security of the people. Surely God would visit them again through the human figure of the Messiah (the anointed one), a "righteous Branch springing forth from David, who would execute justice and righteousness in the land" (Jer. 33:15), bring the people back from exile, restore the nation, and secure

19

Jerusalem once more as God's holy city. But the timing of these mighty events, sometimes called "The Day of the Lord," was not predictable from human referents. They would occur in God's time and at God's initiative, which meant that the faithful were enjoined to wait and watch in hope. So the prophet Habakkuk declared:

> I will take my stand to watch,
>   and station myself on the tower,
> and look forth to see what he will say to me,
>   and what I will answer concerning my complaint.
> And the Lord answered me:
> "Write the vision;
>   make it plain upon tablets,
>   so he may run who reads it.
> For still the vision awaits its time;
>   it hastens to the end—it will not lie.
> If it seem slow, wait for it;
>   it will surely come, it will not delay."
>   —Habakkuk 2:1-3

The prophetic hope of God's coming in the Messiah was fulfilled in Jesus Christ, the anointed one. In Jesus the promise became flesh, and through Jesus, God opened the kingdom of heaven and the final chapter of human history. But Jesus, when he spoke of how the end would come, reiterated the prophetic emphasis: "But of that day or that hour, no one knows, not even the angels in heaven, nor the Son, but only the Father. Take heed, watch; for you do not know when the time will come. . . . And what I say to you I say to all: Watch!" (Mark 13:32-33, 37). Yes, despite certain preliminary indicators that Jesus outlined, the exact timing always remains with God.

Watching and waiting continue to be threshold experiences in our spiritual quest and journey of faith, even as they are part of life itself. No one can avoid them. To each of us come experiences and intersections where we must watch and wait. We wait for the answer, the verdict, the outcome. We wait for school to begin, for weddings to take place, for babies to be born. We watch for the mailman and for the plane's arrival. We wait for the telephone to ring, for Christmas morning, for the doctor's diagnosis, for the word of promotion, for the storm to end, for the pain to ease, and for the light to come.

Scientists wait for the results of the experiment. Farmers wait for the harvest. Space crews and technicians wait for the launch and then the final orbit to be reached. Photographers wait for just the right light and the right composition. Novelists wait for words that will develop characters and delineate plot. Bakers wait for dough to rise and, in lonely forest lookout towers, rangers watch for the first sign of a fire.

Children wait for summer and teenagers wait for their drivers' licenses. Parents wait through all kinds

21

of vigils and crises. And sometimes we even wait to die.

Watching and waiting are part of life. When we keep the called-for vigil, we are better prepared for the answer or the meaning when it comes. That is why waiting expectantly prepares us to receive the revelation of Advent. Knowing how such revelation has occurred in the past makes us anticipate more its happening again. Such awareness is why we enter into the Advent season. During Advent we look back to God's coming in the Christ Child born in Bethlehem and we are better awakened to God's coming among us now. We look back with wonder and are thrust forward with hope to God's final coming in glory. As Henri Nouwen put it, "By conserving the memory of our Christ's birth, I can progress to the fulfillment of his kingdom."

During Advent we look back and behold the light that shattered the darkness at Jesus' birth, and we then follow him as the light of the world, assured that he will lead us out of our darkness and shadows. By looking back and beholding the love that God wrapped up in the Christ Child born at Bethlehem, we are moved to receive God's love in Christ now, to make him the center of our lives, and to let God perfect divine love in our relationships of affirmation and caring. Looking back at God's salvation promise in the mystery of the Incarnation, we claim that promise for our own salvation now and live from hope with courage and dignity, even in the face of evil forces that would violate and destroy, distort and exploit human life and this earth.

Albert Schweitzer proclaimed the importance of expectant waiting: "So I tell you, don't let your hearts grow numb. Stay alert. It is your soul which matters. . . ."

Schweitzer spoke the truth. We must take care not to let the world's deceit lead us to think otherwise. Too much is at stake. We watch and wait. We look back with wonder in order to live now with courage and to look forward with hope. We ponder the mystery of God's coming and ask, "Why did he come? Where did he come? How did he come? Why did he come when he came? What does his coming mean for me and for the world?" We keep vigil at Bethlehem, that we may hold God's light in Christ against the present darkness, that we may stand for truth, share his love with those who have given up on love, and live in eternity's sunrise. To be ready, to be on alert, to be expectant, and to be spiritually alive, we enter into this holy season and keep the feast.

Watching and Waiting Expectantly

For Reflection and Study

1. The Book of Habakkuk belongs to the years of Assyrian decline at the end of the seventh century B.C. The prophet's complaints concern God's silence before the human suffering, moral decay, and collapse of the nation (1:2, 4). Habakkuk voices the question which has been on the lips of every generation, "Why, O Lord? What on earth are you doing? Why must we suffer?" When God's immediate reply is incomplete, the prophet mounts his watchtower. Then comes God's answer, which is recorded in 2:2-3.

   Rewrite God's answer to Habakkuk in your own words. Has this ever been God's word for you? Is it a word that satisfies? For how long?

2. In your group (or in your personal journal here) share a crisis experience when waiting and watching was your only recourse under the circumstance. Do you remember what feelings emerged for you? Why are we impatient at such moments? Why is such waiting so often for us a time of fear and anxiety? Write enough to capture your thoughts.

3. The scripture reading from the Book of Jeremiah comes from a series of announcements of salvation and restoration, which, according to the text, were written by the prophet while he was still imprisoned in the court of the guard (33:1). This section may be a later addition, however, since 33:14-16 is almost an exact quotation of 23:5-6. Whatever its original source, it articulates the prophetic theme of messianic hope. You may want to refer to other such announcements: Isaiah 7:14-15, 9:2-7, 11:1-3, 52:7-10, 61:1-4;

26

Micah 5:2-4; Zechariah 9:9-10; Malachi 3:1-3, 4:1-5. From careful reading of these passages, what do you learn about the longed-for Messiah? What was his role to be? What were the people to do until he came?

4. When Jesus announced that "the time is fulfilled, and the kingdom of God is at hand" (Mark 1:15), what was he telling the people about the messianic hope they held? How was Jesus' messianic fulfillment different from that described by the Hebrew prophets?

5. Contrast Jesus' word in Mark 13 about the end
    time to the detailed predictions made today by
    certain so-called preachers of prophecy and re-
    lated groups who emphasize signs of the end
    and issue warnings of the same. What was Jesus'
    repeated teaching about our response to God's
    final consummation of human history? (You
    may want to refer to Matthew 13:24-30; 24:36-44
    and Luke 17:20-37; 21:29-37.)

6. How have you translated the meanings you
    have discovered in Jesus' birth into your life
    today? Record here and then share with the
    group one or two changes that have occurred in
    your life because of this.

Chapter Two _____

Jesus Came—and Comes!

When all things began, the Word already was. The Word dwelt with God, and what God was, the Word was. . . . So the Word became flesh; he came to dwell among us.

—John 1:1, 14 (NEB)

Read: *Malachi 3:1-2; John 1:1-18; Hebrews 1:1-4*

Have you ever seen something at a distance, such as a cloud formation in the sky, an animal in the brush, or a landmark on the horizon and, having seen it, wanted to show it to others, to have them see it too? You tell them about it and they reply, "Show me! Show me!" You try. You describe where it is and attempt to locate it for them using identifying referents. You even point to it, but still they don't see it. You try again, make the referents more definite and the location more precise. And if they still do not see it, you may even take their heads and adjust them to the right level or angle and point them in the right direction. Still they say, "Show me! Show me!"

The scriptures reveal that God had such a problem with the Hebrew people. In various modes and with different strategies, God tried to show the people how to find the way to life, how to realize their destiny, how to participate in God's purpose, and how to behold the beauty of God's presence. The Bible narrates how God kept trying while the people kept saying, "Show me! Show me!" God led them out of bondage, took them to the promised land, raised up leaders, and sent them prophets to speak the truth. Still the people could not see—or refused to look. Then God sounded the promise of a special messenger, the Messiah, who would come to them and whose name would be called "Wonderful

Counselor, Mighty God, / Everlating Father, Prince of Peace" (Isa. 9:6). This Messiah would be God's revealer and redeemer and through him the people would finally see and understand, return and be saved. In the Messiah, God would inaugurate on earth a reign of peace, justice, and righteousness for all people.

"But in whom?" the people asked. God gave the answer in the Judean village of Bethlehem, even as the prophet Micah had foretold (Mic. 5:27), and Jesus was born to the carpenter Joseph and his wife, Mary, from Nazareth in Galilee. In the human person of Jesus, God wrapped up what God willed and wanted the people to see and to receive, to behold and to enliven. So the writer of Hebrews declared:

In many and various ways God spoke of old to our fathers by the prophets; but in these last days he has spoken to us by a Son, whom he appointed the heir of all things, through whom also he created the world. He reflects the glory of God and bears the very stamp of his nature, upholding the universe by his word of power.

—Hebrews 1:1-3

The cadences of the Proglogue to the Gospel of John also sing with awe of the mystery of the Incarnation:

In the beginning was the Word, and the Word was with God, and the Word was God. . . . And the Word became flesh and dwelt among us, full of grace and truth; we have beheld his glory, glory as of the only Son from the Father. . . . No one has ever seen God; the only Son, who is in the bosom of the Father, he has made him known.

—John 1:1, 14, 18

Not only in his ministry, his teachings, and his acts of healing and exorcism, but more profoundly in his person and his unconditional love for others, Jesus lived out the revelation and the promise of God. While the disciples might not have seen or understood, they sensed about Jesus a divine power and authority. While people like John the Baptist might have asked, "Are you he who is to come, or shall we look for another?" (Matt. 11:3), and while the religious establishment might have disdained him as a teacher who went too far, others recognized God in him and were drawn to him. His death on the cross was perceived by most as refutation of his claims, but his own dying word was "It is finished" (John 19:30)—not a word of defeat, but a word of completion. The centurion at the foot of the cross was so moved by what he saw and experienced in Jesus that he said, "Truly, this was the Son of God!" (Matt. 27:54).

Then came the third day with God's resounding

33

validation in Jesus' resurrection, an event which has continued in persons' lives ever since, prompting them to exult with the Apostle Paul: "For it is the God who said, 'Let light shine out of darkness,' who has shone in our hearts to give the light of the knowledge of the glory of God in the face of Christ" (2 Cor. 4:6). When the world cries out with Philip, "Lord, show us the Father, and we shall be satisfied," Jesus replies by drawing near as a living presence for us and says, "He who has seen me has seen the Father; . . . the Father who dwells in me does his works. Believe me that I am in the Father and the Father in me" (John 14:8, 9, 10-11).

It was God's genius of self–revealing to come in Jesus Christ with a depth of divine love that would go to any length to reach people, to grace them with whole-making power, and to open to them life with eternal possibilities. It was God's strategy of salvation to enter human history in the human form of Jesus who embodied the *shalom*—the justice, peace, and righteousness of God's purpose—and who broke down the dividing walls of estrangement between persons and God, reconciling them to God, to each other, and to themselves. Not only in eternal laws and in the created universe did God reveal the divine purpose, but also with a near–presence in the familiar, living example of Jesus. God not only thundered the word from Mount Horeb but also pronounced the Word intimately in a human life with a flesh-and-blood identity.

God came in Jesus—and comes to us today—because God knew a familiar example is always the most effective definition and the best mode of communication. As Van A. Harvey said, "Human beings only seem to decide concerning the truth about life in general when they are confronted by *a* life in particular." No academic theory, written word, or spoken admonition is ever as convincing or illuminating as a person who embodies and lives out before our very eyes what we seek to know and become. That is why apprenticeship and "on-the-job training" are imperative. That is why the quality of family life and the integrity of parent-child relationships are so determinative of our response to life, our value systems, and our capacity for mature relationships.

What would our best response be if someone asked us what love is, what it means? Should we recommend a textbook or a classic novel about love? Should we suggest going to a philosopher or a psychiatrist for a lecture or dialogue about love? Should we show a Hollywood movie or a TV soap opera? Would not our best response be to love the questioner or send that person into the world until he or she met someone, fell in love, and experienced the joy and fulfillment of loving and being loved?

Consider how we can best define the word *mother.* One dictionary definition says simply, "a female parent." True, but not true enough. To best define what *mother* can mean, we place a loving mother in our midst and observe her ways, her care and concern, her belief in and commitment to her children. Or take the word *character*. One dictionary defines it as "the aggregate of features and traits that form the individual nature of some person or thing." True, but not true enough. To begin to understand what *character* means, we seek out a person who has weathered many a crisis and temptation and bears the consequences with dignity, who has strength of commitment that she or he lives out with constancy against pressure and stress, who can be trusted in all seasons. Then we walk with that person and open ourselves to the positive influence of example and gradually learn what character means.

This, likewise, applies to our understanding and response to God. How do we get to know God? How do we find God? Some persons have met God in the world of nature and been moved by the majesty and beauty, the delicate and awesome power of God as manifested in the universe: in an alpine wildflower or in a giant sequoia; in a butterfly wing or in the rugged peaks of the Rocky Mountains; in a winter sunset, a summer dawn, or in the first roses after pruning; in sea life in a tidepool or in the vast canopy of space. Other persons have heard God's word in the scripture and have understood God's being and purpose in the narratives of faith, in the events of sacred history, and in the prophetic utterances recorded in the Bible. Yet, while these are rich resources of faith and revelation, they still can leave us untouched on a deeply personal level and with a wistful yearning for something more.

In order for us to experience and understand God's nature and will on this deeper, more personal level, God gives us Jesus as a living revelation so that when we meet him and know him, we will behold God. As Jesus moves with caring love among persons, they begin to realize that it is such a loving relationship that God wills and wants to occur with them and betwen them. "As the Father has loved me, so I have loved you; abide in my love" (John 15:9).

God also comes to us today through Jesus' living presence in other persons whom we meet and with whom we share life space. When we are loved by others, we better understand how God loves us. As 1 John teaches us: "If you know love, then you know God" (4:8, AP). Yes, we sense God's presence as we share in relationships of love with wife or husband, son or daughter, aunt or nephew; in the love of a friend or colleague; in an encounter with a neighbor or a stranger. The impact, the impress, and the inspiration of pivotal persons in our lives reveal God to us as we meet the Christ who dwells in them. In gratitude for this, one person wrote to a friend: "I cannot think of you for one moment without finding myself thinking of God. In your love, in your smile, in your faith and caring ways, I see God."

Not only do we recognize and better understand God's revelation when God wraps it up in another person, we also respond to the revelation more completely. The living presence of Christ appearing to the disciples motivated them to overcome their fears, move out into the pagan world, and turn it upside down. It was Paul's personal contagion of faith that helped move Timothy to love and serve God. Nothing is more persuasive, more inspiring and motivating than the example of other persons who live out their faith in our midst, who act from courage in taking the risks of love. Watching these persons cope, we no longer question whether it is possible for us to cope. Seeing them endure, we know it *is* possible for us to hang on five minutes longer or five weeks longer or five years longer. Watching them pour themselves out and stand firm against evil and adversity, we know there are wider limits to our perseverance and sacrifice. Entering with them into prayer and the silence of waiting upon God, we sense the source of strength that is theirs, the reason for their pervasive joy; and we ourselves yearn for what they have received.

The cumulative effect of God at work can be seen, for example, in Francis of Assisi. God came to him in the person of Jesus Christ, and Francis was moved to renounce his wealth and aristocratic status in order to live according to the teachings of Jesus. Then through the spirit of Christ in Francis, God confronted Clare and certain young noblemen of Assisi, and before long a community had gathered to show forth Jesus by serving others. Their loving ministry in turn inspired yet others whose commitment then inspired others.

And so it has continued in every generation. Today Mother Teresa serves the forgotten and the dying in Calcutta. Through her living example, God has touched scores of young women from all over the world who now go to serve Christ as she does. Yes, when God wraps up truth and hope for us in another human life, we can understand more clearly and respond more completely to God's will.

That is why God entered human history in Jesus Christ in the miracle of Bethlehem and why Christ comes to us today. The gospel began in friendship— "one loving heart setting another on fire," as Augustine put it. Christmas tells us how it happened 2,000 years ago and how it happens today as God makes the gospel real for us in the presence of the living Christ and in the lives and love of other persons who have been inspired by the power of Christ's presence.

Jesus Came—and Comes!

For Reflection and Study

1. One of the prominent themes of the New Testament concerns how Old Testament narrative and prophecy have been fulfilled and how the Messiah has appeared in Jesus Christ. The Letter to the Hebrews is devoted entirely to that purpose. The opening verses reflect this theme. Why do you think the Hebrew people repeatedly did not respond to God's revelation?

2. The Prologue to the Gospel of John (John 1:1-18) indicates that Jesus is much more than the Messiah. What does it say about him?

3. We learn much about God through Jesus' life, through his ministry among persons, and through his teachings. Specifically, what do you think we learn

—about God's nature?
—about God's plan for the human family?
—about God's concern for individuals?
—about God's judgment and treatment of sin?
—about God's expectations of the faithful believer?
—about God's promise for the faithful believer?
—about God's finale for human history?

4. Can we prove that Jesus is God? If we cannot, where does our certainty of faith rest?

5. Why do you think that the people closest to Jesus failed to perceive who he was?

6. In what special persons has God wrapped up truth and love for you? Record here and share with the group something about one such relationship in your life.

7. What person, more than any other, makes you think of God? Of Jesus?

Chapter Three _____

Where Jesus Came—and Comes

But you, O Bethlehem Ephrathah,
  who are little to be among the clans of Judah,
from you shall come forth for me
  one who is to be ruler in Israel.

—Micah 5:2

Read: *Micah 5:2-4; Acts 9:32-41; Matthew 3:1-12*

If you ever get to Jerusalem, you can walk where King Herod the Great roamed his palace and where the Magi came to inquire of him about the birth of a new king. Herod's palace is gone, but archaeologists can project the size and grandeur of it from the foundations still intact.

Herod had several such palaces, opulent and impressive royal dwellings built by forced labor. There was a winter palace at Jericho with sunken gardens and bathing pools, the extent of which can be seen today. Herod also built a series of fortresses along the borders of the kingdom, and each included palatial living quarters. One was at Masada and another was the Machgerus, where Herod the Great's son, Herod Antipas, had John the Baptist imprisoned and eventually beheaded. These grandiose palaces had mosaic tile floors, heated pools, frescoed walls, and gilded marble columns. The palaces were maintained by a large staff of servants, to be ready at a moment's notice for the arrival of the king and his retinue.

The palaces were symbols of power, wealth, authority, and control. They were frequented by celebrities, the decision-makers, the "in" crowd, the trend-setters, the arbiters of class and style; and also by the opportunists, the fawning sycophants, and eager henchmen working in the background for their moment of glory.

It is not surprising that the visitors from the East, wanting to discover the newborn king, would head for Herod's palace in Jerusalem. Would that not be the place where royalty would be born? But it was not the birthplace of the king they sought. Where would he be found? When Herod asked his seers and priests for clues about such a pretender, they quoted the messianic prophecy of Micah, who in the eighth century B.C. had declared:

> *But you, O Bethlehem Ephrathah,*
>   *who are little to be among the clans of Judah,*
> *from you shall come forth for me*
>   *one who is to be ruler in Israel.*
>   —Micah 5:2

So in Bethlehem, a small village about six miles south of Jerusalem, where King David had been born and grew up 1,000 years before, another child was born. Where, specifically? In Herod's nearby summer palace? No, not in a palace, but in a *cave where animals were stabled. Contrast of contrasts! Paradox of paradoxes! Yet in that paradox lies the truth of where Jesus Christ came and keeps coming today in the midst of our present realities and contradictions.

---

*Authorities differ on whether Jesus was born in a cave or a stable, but all agree he was born in very humble surroundings.

Jesus comes at points of vulnerability and reachability

Jesus often comes to us at those boundary moments of life when we are vulnerable and reachable. He is never intrusive and does not violate our privacy or integrity. Sometimes in our weakest moments, when our attempts at self-sufficiency no longer sustain, Jesus comes. In such intervals, our barriers are lowered, our deeper needs are exposed and finally acknowledged, and our very soul is laid bare. And in our very weakness Jesus finds us and offers us salvation.

A crisis in a significant personal relationship may render us vulnerable. What we had depended on suddenly changes as a friend or loved one abandons us and walks out of our life forever. Or our vulnerability may come in a season of failure and frustration when nothing we do seems to work, when we no longer can control the outcome, and when the consequences overwhelm us. Or it may be a protracted personal illness that upsets our careful timetables and weakens us to the point that we must depend upon the care and help of others, sometimes upon their feeding us or holding us up for a few faltering steps. Or it may come in the shadows of grief when another's death empties our world and nothing matters much in the awful loneliness that consumes us.

Perhaps the vulnerability comes with the realization that we do not want what we have worked so hard to get, that achievement and status have not yielded the hoped-for satisfaction; that marriage has

49

become only a habit; that the future no longer excites us; that life has become for us nothing more than going through the motions; that something terribly important is missing in us and between us and that we have been standing on the sidelines while life and meaning passed us by.

Whatever our vulnerability, it can be the opening through which we finally allow Jesus to enter our lives. Through our pain or confusion or fear, we can be awakened to God's call.

It was such an awakening that John the Baptist sought through his ministry and radical message in the Judean wilderness. He challenged people to admit their need and to repent, to claim God's promise and to be ready to meet the Messiah. As James Carroll says of John in *A Terrible Beauty:* "He was no marginal man, that Baptist. He made his name by calling people in from the margin, in from safety, in from detachment. He called them into the center, into conversion, into repentance, into readiness. He made them wet with his own water, his own fury, his own fountain. *The water's fine,* he hollered; *come on in!*" John the Baptist knew that people would not recognize—let alone receive—the Messiah unless they were reachable and approachable, which is part of what repentance means and why John's preaching called people to it.

An eminent real estate tycoon and community leader in Los Angeles recounts his moment of awakening, which led him to repent and truly accept Jesus as his Savior and Lord:

> I have been a businessman who sought and achieved success and financial power for forty years. I was trained to trust facts and figures and concrete objects that I can see and touch.
>
> But that changed one Christmas Day several years ago when I fainted for the first time in my life. I fainted twice more that night and was rushed by ambulance to one of Los Angeles' finest hospitals. It was quickly diagnosed that I was hemorrhaging internally. Blood transfusions were administered. Four days later I was still bleeding and exploratory surgery was planned. Then my blood pressure dropped, my heartbeat slowed, I became deathly chilled, lost consciousness and felt I was dying.
>
> When I regained consciousness, I opened my eyes and saw my pastor next to me praying for me. I began to pray along with him. Suddenly and clearly I saw Jesus standing on the opposite side of my bed. I felt a warmness run through my body, and I was overcome with a sense of well-being such as I had never felt before. I reached out my hand to the side of the bed where Jesus stood and felt his hand clasp mine. A week later I was released from the hospital after dozens of X-rays had been taken and every exploratory test known to medical science had been made. Nothing could be found. While I cannot explain it, I believe the Lord Jesus touched me, and now I know what it means to be fully alive.

Yes, Jesus comes today where we are vulnerable, where barriers fall away and we are reachable.

THE UNSETTLING SEASON

Jesus also comes today <u>where people take risks</u> of <u>faith and act boldly</u> in scorn of consequence. We are vulnerable then, also, as we give up being in control and entrust ourselves and the outcome to God. I think that is why Jesus declared: "If anyone would come after me, let him deny himself and take up his cross and follow me" (Matt. 16:24). If we want to experience the persuasion of Christ's presence, we must be willing to hazard the challenge of going the second mile, of loving our enemies, of setting at liberty those who are oppressed, of proclaiming release to the captives, of making peace, of feeding the hungry, and of casting out those modern-day demons that possess and tyrannize our world. If we want to know the power of Jesus with us and within us, we must live our *yes* to whatever summons or task he calls us. As Dag Hammarskjöld put it, "Only one feat is possible—not to have run away."

The Apostle Paul did not run away, even in the most desperate of circumstances, and he could proclaim, "I count everything as loss because of the surpassing worth of knowing Christ Jesus my Lord" (Phil. 3:8).

The monk Telemachus did not run away. Instead, with incredible courage, he challenged the bloody and inhuman gladiatorial games at Rome by one day jumping down into the arena to separate the contestants. We can imagine him shouting, "In the name of God, stop this madness!" The angry spectators dragged him to the center of the arena and stoned him to death. But his witness so moved the Emperor Honorius that soon the ruler banned the gladiatorial games throughout the empire.

In the nineteenth century, Elizabeth Fry did not run away but instead said yes to Christ's call and mounted a one-woman crusade to humanize prisons in England. It was a lonely struggle, marked by villainy and ridicule, but she endured because she sensed Jesus beside her.

Similar stories have been written in our world by the lives of persons who have taken the risks of faith and embodied the gospel, who have told of how Jesus came to them with assurance and courage. From Alan Boesak and Beyers Naudé in South Africa to Joseph Parker in Northern Ireland and Dorothy Day in New York City, from persons trying to reconcile street gangs in Los Angeles to famine workers trying to feed the hungry in the drought-stricken areas of Africa, from medical workers in Central America to refugee workers in Pakistan, the testimony is undiminished. Jesus draws near to them, empowering them with his presence to carry on the work of the kingdom with passionate hope.

Jesus always offered simple but costly solutions to complex human dilemmas, solutions arrived at by some definite action—lifting up the crippled to walk again, advocating the giving away of one's wealth to the poor, going up to Jerusalem, cleansing the Temple, healing on the Sabbath, taking his place with the outcasts and the condemned, touching a leper, dying on the cross. To experience his inspiring and empowering presence is to involve ourselves in the world as he did. It is to give ourselves in love to humanize the structures and eliminate the stigmas of our day. It may mean being lifted up like our Lord—not for praise or rewards, but to suffering and rejection—and finding him beside us in the struggle.

A story set amid the ongoing anguish in present day Chile is both a poignant and dramatic example of where Christ comes today. A Christian named Victor Jara was one of the best known folk singers in Chile. He wrote many songs that captured the imagination and inspired those who struggled for their freedom. In one of the turbulent turnovers in government in 1973, he was arrested and detained with thousands of others in the Chile Stadium in Santiago. When he took his guitar and began to sing, hundreds joined him. The authorities, sensing the threat he posed, broke his hands and later tortured and executed him. But his example and the message of his songs continue to inspire the people of Chile in their prayers and perseverance for freedom and justice. In such acts of faith and courage as Victor Jara showed, Jesus comes.

Jesus also comes today where, in love, people help one another, affirm one another, want what is best for one another and work to make this possible. Where people create beauty in the world, Jesus comes. Where love grows and transforms the wil-

54

Jesus comes where people help one another, affirm & want what is best for ch othe

derness of alienation, injustice, indignity, and exploitation, Jesus comes. Where persons nurture their loyalty and commitment to each other, where persons reach out with constancy of caring, where persons cherish and reverence each other, Jesus comes. And his coming is like the light of six million sunrises, dispelling the darkness of human brokenness and pain and revealing the beauty of our coming together and being together. Where Jesus comes, love is there; and where love is, beauty abides, even in the most barren of human landscapes. As Robert McAfee Brown said: "Where there is beauty apparent, we are to enjoy it; where there is beauty hidden, we are to unveil it; where there is beauty defaced, we are to restore it; where there is no beauty at all, we are to create it." When we love others as Christ loved us, he comes and beauty breaks through with joy.

I have witnessed this miracle happen in a shelter for homeless men on West Madison Avenue in Chicago. There the caring concern of staff members provided the point of glad return for a young architect who was reunited with God and his family and regained his professional stature. I have been blessed by the beauty that emerged in the tortured, lonely soul of a young woman who found a place in a church support group. Not only did she find a place, she also found a reason to keep on living. Through the love of her new friends, she found it possible to believe God loved and accepted her. I

55

remember a special night when everyone in that support group was overcome by Jesus' presence in our midst as we celebrated this young woman's spiritual assurance in Christ. The tears that filled everyone's eyes were tears of joy.

Dr. Richard Babb, in the *Journal of the American Medical Association*, tells his unforgettable story.

I considered myself one of the best and brightest. Having just left a prestigious residency and fellowship program, I thought that I was honed to a fine medical edge. My first law of medical practice (more were certain to come) was soon declared: *A wheelchair outside the treatment room door means trouble and should be avoided at all costs.*

Nonetheless, I violated that law one day, and after taking a deep breath, I stepped over a wheelchair, opened a door, and met John. He was a referral from a colleague, and I was silently furious because John, age 14 years, had cerebral palsy, was painfully deformed, and was extremely ill. He had been abandoned by his parents at an early age, knew few friends, and lived in a foster home. And there he was in my treatment room!

John had widespread cancer. During the next year, numerous and prolonged hospitalizations were required to keep him partially comfortable. He never complained and showed uncommon courage; nonetheless his care became an increasing ordeal.

Finally, after a particularly frustrating day for the two of us, John grabbed my arm and said, "I'm sorry to be such a burden."

That night he died.

I've never forgotten John and the lesson he taught me. It's found in the Gospel according to Luke 14:12-14.

I believe that in ministering to John this young doctor met Jesus, and in that meeting he was reminded of the words of Jesus: "When you give a dinner or a banquet, do not invite your friends or your brothers, or your kinsmen or your rich neighbors, lest they also invite you in return, and you be repaid. But when you give a a feast, invite the poor, the maimed, the lame, the blind, and you will be blessed, because they cannot repay you. You will be repaid at the resurrection of the just."

When Jesus was born 2,000 years ago, his presence filled a cave outside the village of Bethlehem, confounding official religious authorities and their expectations about the Messiah. He comes today in the most unlikely places, confounding those who are religious and surprising those who may not be religious at all. He comes to us all at those boundary moments of life when we are vulnerable and reachable. He draws near when we take the risks of faith and act boldly in scorn of consequence to serve the kingdom. And he also comes when we love and care for each other and when we bring beauty to bleak places of the heart.

Where Jesus Came—and Comes

For Reflection and Study

1. The prophet Micah is identified as a contemporary of Isaiah and active in Judah before the fall of the Northern Kingdom in 722 B.C. In his prophetic judgments, he showed sympathy for the poor of the land and took to task the corruption and cruelty of the institutions and leaders of his nation. His oracles of harsh judgment were balanced by messianic prophecies of hope and redemption where he envisioned the time when a new ruler would shepherd his people as in the days of old. (See chapters 4, 5, and 7 in the Book of Micah.) Micah's words (in 5:2-4) reiterate how the Messiah would come from the line of David, whose city was, of course, Bethlehem. What imagery in this passage reminds you both of David, and of Jesus? Why was it significant that Jesus was born in Bethlehem?

2.   If John the Baptist's task was to prepare people for the Messiah (Matt. 3:1-12), what did his style of ministry and his message do to prepare them? Is such preparation of persons still necessary today in order for them to receive Jesus Christ?

3.   How did Peter's ministry prepare people to meet and receive Jesus? (See Acts 9:32-41 for an example.)

4. Why do you think the author states that Jesus comes to us today where we are vulnerable and reachable? Has that been your experience when Jesus came to you?

5. What does taking a "risk of faith" mean to you? Share in your group examples of people taking such risks. Why do you think Jesus comes to people in such moments?

6. Why might Jesus draw near when people reach out in love to serve other persons and encourage them? Share in your group examples of such Christlike caring that you have witnessed or received, or that you yourself have given to others.

Chapter Four ───────────

How Jesus Came—and Comes

She gave birth to her first-born son and wrapped him in swaddling cloths, and laid him in a manger, because there was no place for them in the inn.

—Luke 2:7

Read: *Isaiah 7:14, 9:2-7; Luke 2:1-20; Philippians 2:5-11*

A Southern California church stages an annual million-dollar extravaganza that it calls "The Glory of Christmas" and advertises it as "recapturing the *simplicity* of the first Christmas." Many of us hail the birth of Jesus with conspicuous consumption, during which we spend enormous amounts of money on glittering gifts and luxuries for persons who have everything.

We like to be dazzled and entertained, do we not? We like to have our senses galvanized with spectacle and unusual exhibitions. In fact, there are now firms which specialize in providing such events and programs. There are experts in motivational research and public relations who insist that they can influence and shape public opinion, that they can create images that are believable and sellable. You can engage them to market a new product, improve your public image, devise a political campaign, design a media blitz, and stage a festive opener with great hoopla.

One wonders why God did not use a few special effects and image boosters when Jesus was born. Yes, I know a brilliant star appeared—but not many knew why or for whom. Yes, I know there was an angel chorus, but no one other than a few poor, nomadic shepherds heard them. I mean, why didn't God let loose a miracle or two like those that oc-

65

curred at the dawn of Creation or with Noah and the flood or with Moses and the Exodus? Not even Hollywood or Madison Avenue could begin to approximate those stunning moments. Moreover, why didn't God choose Athens, Rome, Alexandria—or at least Jerusalem—as the locale for Christ's birth? Why didn't God choose a place where the people were and where the maximum exposure would be gained? Why a cave as the setting? Surely this was not very believable for the birth of the world's Savior and the turning point in humankind's spiritual quest.

Even the prophet Isaiah, who announced the coming of the Messiah King, added the promise that the virgin's child so destined would finally sit in royal splendor on David's throne. That is why the actual birth of Jesus was so surprising with its inconspicuous setting, its simplicity and reticence. And yet this very anomaly in Jesus' birth reveals how Jesus comes today into the midst of our lives, in our time and our town.

He came at first with gentle sign, and so he still comes. A young working-class couple welcomes their first child in a cave with its pungent odors, among animals whose moist eyes reflect the flickering light of the oil lamps brought in for the birth. No pomp, no fine appointments, no coverage by the media. Just the quiet rustle of animals, the familiar human sounds heard at any birth, and the cry of a new baby who was then laid in a manger as his first crib. . . . Here was God's gentle sign of incarnate love.

Jesus called for gentle ways among his followers, nowhere more memorable than when he counseled them: "If any one strikes you on the right cheek, turn to him the other also. . . . Love your enemies and pray for those who persecute you" (Matt. 5:39, 44). He also told them: "Blessed are the meek, for they shall inherit the earth. . . . Blessed are the meriful, for they shall obtain mercy" (Matt. 5:5, 7).

We need a gentle sign that respects individual integrity and honors personal privacy, that treats human feelings with care, that reverences personal worth and is premised on understanding and empathy. We need a gentle sign that beckons and inspires, that attracts and affirms our human stature and dignity. When we are coerced or manipulated, we become mere puppets—pawns and robots with servile minds and feckless wills.

The world, of course, argues otherwise. We live in a day when aggressive and assertive ways are touted while reticence and deference are ridiculed. Examine the self-improvement section of your nearest bookstore and you will find whole shelves filled with books with titles like *The Act of Getting Your Own Sweet Way, Look Out for #1, The Virtue of Selfishness, Competitive Advantage, How To Get What You Really Want*. These titles seem to suggest that you ought to get what you want, even if you have to use or misuse other people; let nothing stand in your way as you move toward your self-centered satisfactions—not your own conscience, other people's feelings, religion, traditional principles, or altruistic impulses. So society applauds the coercive ones, lionizes the ruthless ones, and almost canonizes the deceptive ones—those who lie and cheat and defraud with impunity. In many films and tv shows, such characters are written in scripts as the strongest and portrayed as the real heroes.

Yet on the sundown side of the day when the hurrahs are but an echo, the deals are all made, the battles have been fought, and the prizes have tarnished, whom does history affirm? Make the question more personal and ask who do we want beside us when we must go through a crisis? With whom do we want to share our joy and sorrow in intimate moments of trust and caring? Do we really want the clever manipulator, the swaggering achiever, the arrogant conqueror, the assertive handler who acts as if he or she knows what is best for everyone else?

On his seventieth birthday, the great healer and scientist Louis Pasteur was honored at a jubilee celebration in the amphitheater of the Sorbonne. In the appreciation speech he prepared for the occasion, Pasteur wrote that "nations will unite, not to destroy, but to build, and that the future will belong to those who have done most for suffering humanity." Yes, the future will belong to strong but gentle people like Albert Schweitzer, Mohandas Gandhi, Dorothy Day, Edith Cavell, Toyohiko Kagawa,

Helen Keller, Jean Vanier, Archbishop Oscar Romero, Mother Teresa of Calcutta, and Martin Luther King, Jr. In a letter to Albert Schweitzer, Martin Buber wrote, "I have always been concerned with those who help mankind, and you have been one of the great helpers in so many ways. Every time one [person] helps another, the *hasidim* say, an angel is born."

Around the time of the birth of Jesus, how would we have looked for the world's hope to be revealed? On whom would we have bet in the power struggles and upheavals of that day? Herod, who called himself "The Great"? Quirinius in his quarters as Roman legate of Syria? Caesar in his palace on the Palatine Hill in Rome? Or a working-class couple with their firstborn son in a rude cave in the unpromising village of Bethlehem that was part of Palestine, disdained as the backwash of the Roman Empire?

We need a gentle sign that seeks our best and deepest response while at the same time one that affirms our worth regardless of our response. So God, in a quiet, gentle way, "came down the backstairs at Bethlehem, lest he blind us by excess of light" (George Buttrick). And this small town, Bethlehem, was where a child was born who would beckon and enable, save and restore through the power of love. Still today Jesus comes in ways that the world deems powerless and ineffective. He comes in unheralded, unnoticed ways that do not make the front page of the newspaper or the

6-o'clock news but that leave his indelible mark on the lives of persons who welcome and receive him. In those who say yes to his presence, a Christlike spirit is born, which soon becomes quiet human deeds of constancy and gentle strength.

An Associated Press news article told the story of a nurse who embodied that gentle strength. She worked in the psychiatric ward of the VA Hospital at Coatesville, Pennsylvania. At lunchtime patients privileged to leave locked wards went to the main dining room. For the sixty or so left in the wards, there was a small dining facility where food was delivered from the main kitchen. These wards had one nurse and two orderlies to get the seriously disturbed patients through a meal. Six hands were inadequate.

One day at lunchtime a toilet had overflowed, and the nurse made some effort to clean it up. But she had to keep her eye on five patients in wheelchairs along with a dozen others clamoring for her attention. Three times in twenty minutes she walked past a patient lying curled in the corner before she could stop and with a smile help him to his feet.

A visitor asked the nurse, "Doesn't this ever depress you?"

"Not really," the nurse answered. Then she added, "If I begin to feel depressed I just remember that the hospital staff is among the few people in the world who care what happens to these men. In some cases we're the only ones who do."

Jesus came as gentle sign, and still he comes today where loving people act in gentle ways from great strength, where people see possibility and respond quietly with skill, kindness, generosity, and courage.

Jesus also came as a lowly sign, and still he comes where people admit their need and limitations, where there is an underlying sense that whatever power or gifts they may have are not so much in them as through them. Jesus reminded his followers that such a response was to be theirs: "Whoever exalts himself will be humbled, and whoever humbles himself will be exalted" (Matt. 23:12). He also told the Disciples: "You know that those who are supposed to rule over the Gentiles lord it over them, and their great men exercise authority over them. But it shall not be so among you; but whoever would be great among you must be your servant, and whoever would be first among you must be slave of all" (Mark 10:42-44).

In the Sermon on the Mount Jesus encapsulated this teaching in one of the beatitudes, "Blessed are the poor in spirit" (Matt. 5:3), which might be translated *Blessed are the humble-minded*. Jesus also taught that the "first will be last, and the last first" (Matt. 19:30).

But Jesus' teachings and his spirit are often disdained today by a world that treats privilege, position, and self-aggrandizement as the authentic measure of greatness and power; that overuses the

71

superlative to define importance; that still is particular about rank and order, status and prominence. Most persons one meets would not appreciate being characterized as humble or meek. Most would take serious objection to being a servant to anyone. (Although those same persons may be more slave to their jobs, their life-styles, and their image-keeping than they realize.) Most people dismiss Jesus' teachings and his spirit as impractical and visionary as a means of dealing with the ambiguities and competitive struggles of business and profession, of politics and international relations.

It is very apparent that the world's ways of spurious pride, competitive outguessing, and status-seeking render us less than human and leave us unfulfilled. The stresses and pressures of staying on the defensive, "getting the biggest bone," and overpowering someone else have contributed to neuroses, troubled marriages and divorces, abused children, health problems, the arms race, the drug binge, and a host of other problems that blight the quality of life, distort love, and reduce human stature.

What we need, in truth, is the humble-minded, unpretentious, God-centered life that Jesus lived and to which he summons us. We need his lowly sign that awakens our goodness, restores our true dimension, and moves us toward community, responsibility, and reverence for God. We need a sign that draws near with the contagion of inspiration and influence, that rouses and points us to claim wholeness and a life that is fit for living, fit for dying, and fit for a destiny beyond both.

God gave us a sign when Jesus took upon himself the form of a servant. The Apostle Paul's matchless words celebrate this truth: "Have this mind among yourselves, which is yours in Christ Jesus, who, though he was in the form of God, did not count equality with God a thing to be grasped, but emptied himself, taking the form of a servant, being born in the likeness of men. And being found in human form he humbled himself and became obedient unto death, even death on a cross" (Phil. 2:5-8).

Jesus, whose first cradle was a cow's eating trough, said that he came not to be ministered unto, but to minister. Whether taking children into his arms, placing his hands on the unseeing eyes of the blind or on the numb legs of the paralyzed, feeding the hungry, listening to the wistful yearnings of the powerful and wealthy; whether drawing near the tormented or kneeling before his Disciples to wash their feet, the love in his humble ways was revealing and transforming. He challenged his followers then, and still he challenges this age. His ways are so simple! His spirit is so liberating! His strength and power are so direct and yet so reticent. "He will not break a bruised reed / or quench a smoldering wick" (Matt. 12:20). His life showed no mock heroics but instead was a life which (in our clearer moments we know) is once and for all what life is all about, what God created it to be.

The wealth of empire, the strength of military force and conquering armies, celebrity status, and triumphal arches, winning by intimidation, and elbowing our way to the top—are these the measure of our humanity, the mark of greatness, the evidence of power? No, the sign for all times is in a cave where a child is born whose name is Jesus, who took the form of a servant to reveal the love that saves us and keeps us.

How Jesus Came—and Comes

For Reflection and Study

1. The reference from Philippians 2:5-11 is often called the kenotic passage, from the Greek word *kenosis* which means "to pour out or empty" (verse 7). As you study the passage, try to put into your own words what Paul is saying about Jesus and how he fulfilled God's salvation plan for us. You may want to share your interpretation in your group.

2. In the messianic passage from Isaiah 7:14 and
    9:2-7, the reference to "a virgin shall conceive
    and bear a son" and to "for to us a child is born"
    tie the prophet's words to the birth of Jesus.
    Read the passages out loud in your group and
    then share what emotions and images they
    evoke. How would you compare them with the
    images in the Philippians 2:5-11 passage? Make
    notes here.

3. Do you agree with the author when he says we
    need a gentle and a lowly sign? Are the argu-
    ments convincing? Does a gentle and lowly sign
    fit in our world? Why or why not?

4. Were Jesus to be born in America today, where do you think the event might occur? Do you think we would pay attention if someone told us about it? Write a few sentences here and then discuss your response in the group.

5. Who is the most powerful person living today? If we in this country were to vote on our choice for the greatest American, who do you think would win? For whom would you vote?

6. Do you have any difficulty following Jesus by being a servant? Do you believe that you can follow Jesus and still seek status and deference?

Chapter Five _____

When Jesus Came—and Comes

And [Gabriel] came to her and said, "Hail, O favored one, the Lord is with you!" But she was greatly troubled at the saying, and considered in her mind what sort of greeting this might be.

—Luke 1:28-29

Read: *Isaiah 11:1-9; Galatians 4:4-7; Luke 1:26-35*

Arriving early for a visit or a dinner party can cause more problems than being late. I well remember a certain dinner invitation where I mistakenly showed up an hour or so earlier than had been planned. Everyone involved now can joke about the event in retrospect, but it was no laughing matter for the embarrassed and flustered hosts on the day it happened. The vacuum cleaner sat in the middle of the living room floor, the son in the family was bathing the dog in the bathtub, the hostess's hair was still in curlers, the host had just come in from cleaning the stable, and to "untop" it all, the cake for dessert had somehow slid from its cooling rack and lay flattened on the floor. Ever since then, I always doublecheck the appointed time when I am expected to arrive for a dinner party or any other social event. It is not only courteous, it also is merciful!

While we may monitor our social calendar to avoid surprises and interruptions, we cannot do so with life. The contingencies that break upon us in a given day may alter that day and all our tomorrows. As someone put it: "Life is what happens while you're making other plans." Henri Nouwen, in his book *Reaching Out*, quoted a friend as saying, "My whole life I have been complaining that my work was constantly interrupted, until I discovered that my interruptions were my work."

81

We have been taught that the educated person anticipates, makes plans, follows schedules, and stays on track. That is all well and good if you are talking about fixing a leaky roof, conducting a scientific experiment, or paying taxes. But when venturing a dream, making a marriage work, raising children, coping with illness, or climbing a mountain, we are well advised to expect anything to happen, for it will. After a week of treating patients who had lost all hope, a doctor suggested to his pastor that he preach on the subject of "life's immutable law of surprises."

The Bible is certainly replete with surprises, divine interruptions, and unexpected visitations. There is Abraham whose comfortable lifestyle is upset by God's visitation; and there is his wife, Sarah, who becomes pregnant in her old age after so many years of waiting for a child. There is Moses who gets the surprise of his life while hiding out in Midian and young David who is called from watching the family flocks to be anointed king by Samuel. There is Gomer, whose life is turned around at least twice in her relationship with Hosea, and there is Jeremiah, who as a carefree youth is stopped in his tracks and called to be a prophet. There is Mary Magdalene's astonishing encounter with the risen Lord in the graveyard, Peter's amazing vision and summons at Joppa, and Paul's astounding confrontation on the road to Damascus. And there is the hauntingly lovely scene in Nazareth when the young Mary, betrothed to Joseph, is ushered into a shining moment by God's special message, "Hail, O favored one, the Lord is with you! . . . Do not be afraid, Mary, for you have found favor with God. And behold, you will conceive in your womb and bear a son, and you shall call his name Jesus" (Luke 1:28-31).

Yes, the coming of Jesus brought one divine surprise after another—for Mary, for Joseph, for the shepherds, and for the officiary at Jerusalem. His coming broke upon the world in unexpected ways and with uncharacteristic impact. While many should have been prepared, since the advent of the Messiah was a cherished hope among devout Jews, they were looking for a very different turn of events than occurred in Bethlehem. Expectations determine perceptions, and so the people were unprepared for how Jesus would hold the world open for God's possibilities.

If any of us had been in Mary or Joseph's place, we would have understood their startled reaction, for who could be ready for what God asked them to be and do? For the shepherds, caught up in the grim struggle to stay alive and support their families and concerned about too little pasture and too many losses, the divine announcement that interrupted their routine must have seemed exotic against the ordinariness of their days. Small wonder they were shaken and felt almost overwhelmed.

Everyone touched by Jesus' coming would have

preferred advance notice and perhaps a more convenient time, but God's timing does not await a more convenient season. As Paul, who had great insight into how God acts, wrote, "When the time had fully come, God sent forth his Son, born of woman . . . to redeem those who were under the law . . ." (Gal. 4:4-5). There are two Greek words that when translated mean *time: chronos* and *kairos.* *Chronos* is time measured by clock and calendar. *Kairos* is time qualified by meaning and purpose, time that is measured by revelation and fulfillment. So when Paul writes that "the time had fully come," the Greek word is *kairos.* In the New Testament, *kairos* is always God's time, time with a divine dimension and intention.

Jesus came to the world in *kairos* to fulfill God's purpose, which means that human factors and the conditions of the world were not the determining factors, no matter how propitious they may have been. That is why the event at Bethlehem surprised everyone and was overlooked by many.

Still Jesus comes today according to God's purpose and timing and not necessarily according to the devout petitions of the religious or because of a particular crisis in human history. Moreover, when Jesus comes again at the "end time," it will be at God's initiative and not in some year, month, or day calculated by self-appointed prognosticators who have derived their indicators by interpreting certain prophetic references from the Bible. As Jesus himself declared: "For the Son of man is coming at an hour you do not expect" (Matt. 24:44).

Yes, what we have discovered in our own experience the scripture corroborates; namely, God's ways are not our ways and God's purposes transcend our thoughts. As Paul suggested, we only know in part and "now we see in a mirror dimly" (1 Cor. 13:12). That is why, when Jesus comes today, his coming is always at a moment that catches us off guard and takes us by surprise. He comes unannounced. In the midst of some ordinary helter-skelter day we meet him and our world is never the same again.

He may come to us when we struggle to bear our private burden with courage and dignity—some persons have met him there and received strength enough to make it through. He may come to us at the crossroads where we wrestle with a pivotal decision and are not sure we want to make a commitment. So he came to me during a period when I was running away from the call to the ordained ministry. One night he stood at the foot of my bed without a word. His appearance was unlike any artist's likeness I have studied, but his face and the look in his eyes are indelibly etched in my memory.

He may come to us at boundary moments of illness, as he came to the Los Angeles businessman mentioned in chapter 2. I have known other persons who have experienced the sudden touch of Jesus' hand and still others who have beheld him beckoning to them or walking beside them as they coped with their pain and their dying.

Dan McClimon was the very popular track and field coach at the University of Wisconsin until his death in a small-plane crash. Some years before that tragedy, the McClimons' fourth-grade son, Timmy, had died of leukemia. At that time Dan McClimon had quietly shared with friends and colleagues an incident that brought him and his wife, Pat, the strength they needed then:

> As Timmy lay in the hospital, still clear-eyed and bright but nearing the end, Dan said to him, "Don't be afraid, son. The Lord is waiting to hold you." The boy replied, "I know He is, Daddy. Can't you see him? He's standing there beside you."

Jesus may come to us in the midst of a great joy and in moments of celebration. I remember how he surprised a certain couple at their wedding. They had come through a stormy period in their relationship before the wedding and at one point had decided to separate and cancel their wedding plans. In the counseling sessions I spent with them, they struggled with some tough problems. I encouraged them to pray together as they worked through these problems. They did, and slowly new dimensions of love and commitment opened to them.

On their wedding day joy consumed them both. They knelt after taking their vows and I offered a prayer for them, asking God to bless their marriage. As I prayed I could sense them praying with me. After we joined in our Lord's Prayer, they raised their heads. I noticed that they were not so much looking at me but through me with eyes full of light. They whispered something to each other, and when they stood up, they whispered to me that they had both beheld the presence of Jesus in back of me with his hand raised in a blessing. I did not pronounce a benediction—Christ had already given it to them. Instead, the three of us just hugged each other in a moment I will cherish forever.

On several occasions a woman has told me how she experienced Jesus with her in the birth of her baby or when she first held the infant to her breast. Other persons have shared how Jesus joined them in moments of reconciliation and reunion. Athletes have testified how Jesus drew near to them when they gave their all, both in victory and loss.

Jesus may also come to us in the life of another person whose need evokes our caring concern and love, just as that doctor discovered in the young cancer patient he treated whose story was included in chapter 3. That is how Jesus came with surprise to Francis of Assisi in a leper whom Francis was moved to embrace along the road one day. Jesus came to Toyohiko Kagawa in an abandoned sick child of the Shinkawa slums of Kobe, Japan, whom he brought to his little hut and cared for as his son. Mother Teresa tells how she meets Jesus in those whose heads she cradles and whose dignity she restores in their dying. Teachers have met Jesus' surprising presence in vexing students; employers have met Jesus in troublesome employees; salespersons have met Jesus in unlikely customers; and some of us have met Jesus in strangers whose encounter with us left a blessing that we still carry with us.

We never know when Jesus will come to us today. That is why our faith journey is never monotonous or hopeless. When we least expect it, under circumstances that are not conducive, in situations where all possibility is exhausted and hope has died, in hellish settings that contradict all that is meant by love and faith, Jesus comes. He comes in the power of the Resurrection and with the promise of God's love that never lets us go. We are never beyond his saving touch. He will go to any lengths to find us. Nothing can keep him from coming, not even our bad faith or our unfaith.

A December, 1987 column in *Sojourners* magazine captured how this happens:

I wasn't making much progress on a sermon approach when the 8:18 A.M. H-2 bus arrived right on time, a minor miracle of sorts if you know anything about adherence to bus schedules in the District of Columbia. Since it was the day after Christmas, very few people were on the usually crowded bus. In fact the bus was nearly empty, with the exception of some developmentally disabled people who ride the H-2 line on their way to jobs elsewhere in the city. A young woman and a couple of older women sat near the front while three younger men were seated toward the rear. They were busily and happily talking with each other. As the bus moved along its rush-hour route, I continued to think about Simeon and Anna [Luke 2:22-38] against the backdrop of their chatter.

Since my thinking about the sermon was not bearing much fruit, I decided to set the passage aside until another time and listen to the conversations going on between the front and back of the bus. The passengers were very excited and animated as they told each other about their Christmas experiences, what they had given each other, what gifts they had received, what they ate for Christmas dinner, and so on.

As the conversation died down, one of the young men in the back started to softly sing "Silent Night." He had just finished the first verse when one of the women in the front turned to him and harshly scolded him, saying, "Shhh! Shhh! No, no, stop singing that. That's for Christmas. That was yesterday. It's over now." I was somewhat reluctantly agreeing with her logic when the young man ever so gently, but firmly, replied, "No, no, that's not true. It's only just beginning. It's only just beginning."

Jesus comes at unlikely moments in unexpected places—like on city buses—transforming them and us with the power of his presence and the persuasion of God's love!

When Jesus Came—and Comes

For Reflection and Study

1. Isaiah 11:1-9 is the celebrated vision of the savior-king (the Messiah) who will spring forth from the stem of Jesse (King David's lineage) to rule a wide and harmonious universe. The prophet as poet uses rich metaphor to emphasize the wonder of it all: God's spirit nurtures the budding sprout, the sea in its plentitude, the animal/human world in a peaceful relationship, and also soothes the ancient enemy, the serpent. The Messiah rules justly and preserves this Eden-like existence. In what ways does this passage speak of Jesus' birth? What elements of surprise does the vision contain?

2. When God's messenger Gabriel appeared to Mary in Luke 1:26-35, the message he brought was both an announcement/summons and also an assurance. What was the announcement in Gabriel's message? What was the assurance? Would that assurance have allayed your amazement had you been in Mary's place?

3. Some Christians tell you that with prayer they have somehow controlled events, and some are sure they have prevailed upon God to change divine time frames. Have you ever tried to do that? How? Did it work? Do you think our prayers can manipulate God? Can we, through prayer, foresee the future?

4. Has God ever surprised you? In what ways has Jesus' coming into your life brought sudden changes or blessings? Share with your group one such experience.

5. What experiences in your life would you attribute to *kairos*—to God's timing?

Chapter Six _____

Jesus' Coming and Our Going

Awaiting our blessed hope, the appearing of the glory of our great God and Savior Jesus Christ, who gave himself for us to redeem us from all iniquity and to purify for himself a people of his own who are zealous for good deeds.

—Titus 2:13-14

Read: *Isaiah 60:1-2, 19-22; Titus 2:11-15; Matthew 2:1-12*

Every household, I suppose, has a special place where Christmas tree decorations and other seasonal bric-a-brac are stored from year to year. Attics are a favorite place, as are basements. But if you live in a California house without either attic or basement, the rafters of the garage serve the purpose. An annual ritual around December 1 is to dust off the Christmas storage boxes and unpack them. Then after the Christmas holidays the ritual is to repack and seal them, putting them away for another year. Invariably a trinket is overlooked, and so one has to have a satellite storage for the items that didn't quite make the boxes. How the collection grows over the year is incredible, for who can discard a Christmas bauble—especially if Aunt Hannah handmade it or cousin Hugo bought it as a souvenir on his trip to Europe? Certain Christmas decorations turn into miniature time capsules, for in them we enshrine memories and meanings connected with the particular Christmas when they first came into our possession.

Unfortunately, we too often let the meaning of Christmas itself become a memory which we store away along with the decorations year after year. For a brief period of three or four weeks (give or take one or two) the coming of Jesus is something we claim and celebrate. The very thought of the Baby's birth

97

at Bethlehem, the angels singing to the shepherds, and the Wise Men's journey warms the heart, lifts the spirit, and pushes back the encroaching worries and doubts, the problems and hostilities in us and in our world. Colman McCarthy, a columnist for the *Washington Post*, observed that Jesus' birth "was the beginning of an improbable Kingdom" and that in the history of Christianity few people have completely believed in this Kingdom. (Nietzsche said, "In truth, there was only *one* Christian, and he died on the cross.") Further, Mr. McCarthy wrote that Christmas joy is marked by humanity being summoned to celebrate that improbability and to rejoice in the Nativity moment when new possibilities and hopes are given to humanity—when joy and peace arise from the *intention* to begin building the Kingdom.

For many, the intention is about as far as it goes, and too soon the hope and the promise of Christmas dissipate in the clamor and contradictions, the anxieties and alienations of our daily lives. The Christmas celebration comes and then is over and with it fades whatever commitment it may have awakened in us.

The truth, of course, is that Jesus' coming does not end with the calendar or with the festivities or with the final packing-up. His coming is always a beginning and a sending.

Yes, Jesus' coming becomes our going. The hope and promise of his advent are actualized in his mission—to which his coming calls us. Our celebration of Christmas must, therefore, lead to Epiphany's dedication when we "show Christ forth" in our lives by being agents of his love and possibility in the world.[†]

The New Testament makes clear that many persons who responded to Jesus were immediately confronted with a "Go!", whether it was

- the first disciples whom Jesus sent out two by two (Matt. 10:5; Mark 6:7);
- the rich aristocrat to whom Jesus said, "Go, sell what you possess and give it to the poor . . . and come, follow me" (Matt. 19:21);
- the Gerasene demoniac to whom Jesus said, "Go home to your friends, and tell them how much the Lord has done for you, and how he has had mercy on you" (Mark 5:19).

Again and again in the gospel accounts, persons meet Jesus and then they hear an imperative for action:

- "Rise, take up your bed and go home" (Matt. 9:6).
- "You give them something to eat" (Matt. 14:16).
- "Love your enemies" (Matt. 5:44; Luke 6:27).
- "Let your light so shine" (Matt. 5:16).
- "Love one another" (John 15:12).
- "Take, eat; this is my body" (Matt. 26:26).

[†]The word *epiphany* from the Greek is translated "to show forth" or "to manifest."

To be with Jesus was to learn soon enough there was something more that a person was meant to do and to be—a need or a cause one was to serve, a person or persons one was to love, a change one was to make, a task one was to accomplish. Encountering Jesus today is no different. His coming to us becomes our going to others, and the gifts of his presence always include an awareness of where we should be and what we should be about. Or so it has been for me on my faith journey. Jesus' coming to me as a young man ended up in my going into the ordained ministry. Whenever he comes to me, I know I will be asked to take some risks of love—to do the truth, to involve myself in what I perhaps would rather avoid, to accept the unwanted challenge, to put skin on the gospel, and to serve at the crossroads.

I remember how Jesus came to me in a wonderful vision, and before long I was working with troubled teenagers and taking one into our home. I remember once when I told Jesus how much I loved him, he told me to start a social service agency in north San Diego where the helpless and poor could find food, shelter, clothes, medical assistance, and jobs. I remember how, after another ecstatic encounter with Jesus at a retreat, I had to take a stand on fair housing and be impugned and disdained by persons I thought were my friends. I remember a certain Advent season when Jesus' coming to me became my going to the county jail to be with and to walk beside a young teacher and father who had been arrested on child molestation charges. I recall how we faced together the calumny by church and community through a long, drawn-out trial before he was cleared of the charges and released.

There are persons I know to whom Jesus has come, and their response has taken them to be volunteer cooks in a shelter for the homeless or to be volunteer workers in an AIDS hospice. Others have become involved in peace efforts and in protests against nuclear testing. In other situations Jesus' coming has given persons the courage to care for a handicapped child or an elderly parent. There are yet others whose love for Jesus is translated into working with street gangs, with youth anti-drug programs, or with environmental causes. Some have placed their lives on the line for racial justice and for the humane treatment of illegal aliens. And some have helped organize centers for abused women and children, shelters for runaway teenagers, and support programs for the mentally ill—all because Jesus came to them in love and sent them out to love others.

Read the testimony of persons like Albert Schweitzer for whom Jesus' coming was Schweitzer's going to Africa, or like Sister Ita Ford whose experience of Jesus led her to Central America where she was brutally murdered as she served among the poor. Hear the testimony of Dr.

Sheila Cassidy, whose love for Jesus became for her a missionary journey to Chile. There she treated the gunshot wounds of a revolutionary leader and ended up in prison herself, held incommunicado without charge for month after month after month. Read the testimony of Christopher Eldridge, whose experiences of Jesus became his going to Africa where he works with the Save the Children Fund. He tenaciously refuses to give up despite the miasmic despair that haunts the work. In a December 1985 *New York Times Magazine* article "The Famine Workers," he is quoted as saying, "I intend to stay in this line of work. If I can ease the pain of even one child, I think I have done some good."

Time magazine's December 27, 1982 issue included the moving story of Sister Emmanuelle, 74 years young, who rises each morning at 4:30 A.M. to begin her day as a loving and caring presence among the 10,000 garbage pickers of Cairo, Egypt. The people with whom she lives and whom she serves are considered untouchables "who live in what amounts to perpetual serfdom, bequeathing their trade and squalor to succeeding generations."

The garbage pickers maintain their existence by sorting through the city's refuse that is hauled out in donkey carts. The ragged men and women and children scavenge for bottles and tin cans to sell, and they feed the garbage to their pigs that roam freely in and out of homes. Infant mortality in the area is, not surprisingly, 40 percent.

At 9:00 A.M. each day, Sister Emmanuelle welcomes some forty children to her hut. She teaches both Christians and Muslims to read and write and helps them learn of the wider world beyond the garbage dump. Waving aside the swarms of flies that fill the air as enormous clouds, Sister Emmanuelle spends hours visiting her people, carrying a ledger in which she has carefully recorded the names and needs of 3,000 families. She is gentle, but her gentleness hardens to strong metal when she challenges officials and bureaucrats to do more to help the garbage pickers.

Speaking of her life in the refuse heap of Cairo, Sister Emmanuelle says, "My job is to prove that God is love, to bring courage to these people. . . . I wouldn't want to be anywhere else because here I feel I am giving the life of Jesus Christ to the children."

Jesus' coming is our going, our moving out to those intersections where cross the crowded ways of humanity. His coming is our moving closer in loving ways to give others the life of Jesus and to show Christ forth as God's gift of grace and salvation for all persons.

We are not sent by Jesus to do everything, but we are sent to do something. And in this world where what we do seems so little, the least we dare do is the most we can. What we are called to do may seem beyond us, far exceeding our best gifts and strengths, but we discover, as we engage the struggle, that we are not alone. We discover that what is required of us is bestowed upon us by God in ways that beggar our imaginings. Best of all, we sense Jesus' presence with us.

Martin Luther King, Jr., shared how that awareness redeemed many a desperate moment for him when fatigue, danger, and ugly opposition reduced all hope of continuing in the nonviolent protest movement that sought civil rights and human dignity for black people and moral righteousness for all people. He tells of sitting one night at the kitchen table of his home, trying to recover from a telephone caller's scurrilous threat. He began to pray, asking God to take the burden and telling God he could not go on alone. As he prayed he felt the presence of God in a way he had never before experienced it. King found he could go on, and he did.

We are not sent out by Jesus with all the answers. We are not asked to be brilliant but to be faithful. We may, in fact, be called to do for others what we ourselves need. We may be asked to speak the word we need to hear and to encourage in others what is still unrealized in us. We are "earthen vessels" (2 Cor. 4:7) and unfit to be God's agents, but "by God's grace we are who we are" (1 Cor. 15:10, AP). Since God has in the past summoned and employed many unlikely candidates, we can take heart when Jesus comes to us and sends us out.

At Bethlehem the Three Kings found who they sought, and before long they were headed east with the joy of their discovery. At Bethlehem the shepherds found just what the angels had told them and then headed back to the hills, praising and glorifying God. As with these witnesses to Jesus' birth, for us Jesus' coming is always our going, our going to share what we have been given, to walk in his light and to live out the wonder of his love.

Howard Thurman, former Dean of the Chapel at Boston University, distinguished preacher and well-known author, celebrated this truth in "The Work of Christmas."

> When the song of the angels is stilled,
> When the star in the sky is gone,
> When the kings and princes are home,
> When the shepherds are back with their flock,
> The work of Christmas begins:
> > To find the lost,
> > To heal the broken,
> > To feed the hungry,
> > To release the prisoner,
> > To rebuild the nations,
> > To bring peace among brothers,
> > To make music in the heart.

Epiphany celebrates how Jesus was manifested to the whole world. Epiphany also reminds us that Jesus' coming is always our going, our going to do the work of Christmas, our going to show forth Christ, to be agents of God's possibility, grace, and peace!

Jesus' Coming and Our Going

For Reflection and Study

1. The opening verses of Isaiah 60 contain a great
    poem with light as its theme, for it celebrates the
    day that begins and never ends. The poem de-
    scribes in exquisite language the dawn as light
    over the holy city shining from above against a
    panorama of darkness and articulates the hope
    of the nation for restoration after the Exile—
    "And nations shall come to your light, and kings
    to the brightness of your rising" (Isa. 60:3). Why
    do you think this passage is often used as a text
    for Epiphany? For Christians the passage points
    to Jesus' birth. Why?

2. What meanings do you find in the visit of the
    Wise Men at Jesus' birth, as narrated in the sec-
    ond chapter of Matthew? What do we know
    about these visitors from the East?

3. We have learned that the word *epiphany* comes from the Greek verb meaning "to show forth" or "to manifest." Why do you think this word was chosen by the church to mark the visit of the Wise Men, the first Gentiles to behold the Messiah? (The words from Titus 2:11 may help you answer the question.)

4. Can you think of encounters in the Gospel, other than those mentioned by the author, in which people who met Jesus were sent out with an action imperative?

5. If Jesus has come to you, did his coming become a going for you? Share with the group what you were led to do or whom you were called to serve.

6. What work of Christmas was yours to do last year? What happened because of it? What work of Christmas is yours to do this year?

7. Have you ever felt, like Sister Emmanuelle, that you "gave the life of Jesus" to someone else? Will you share with the group how it happened? Makes some notes here first.

8. Are there persons you know in whom Jesus' coming became a mission that changed her or his life? Who are these persons and what are they doing today?

Prayers for
Advent, Christmas,
and Epiphany

Lord, the calendar calls for Christmas. We have traveled this way before. During this Advent season we would see what we have never seen before, accept what we have refused to think, and hear what we need to understand. Be with us in our goings that we may meet you in your coming. Astonish us until we sing "Glory!" and then enable us to live it out with love and peace. In the name of your Incarnate Word, even Jesus Christ. *Amen.*

God of Hope, the sounds of Advent stir a longing in your people. They reach us in the midst of our routines where we hurry big for little reasons. We hear them even as we give safe answers to questions we do not care to ask. Crumble our walls and make a place in our lives for the freshness of your love, that is well-lived in Jesus Christ and still given to all who confess their need and dare to respond to your Holy Presence. *Amen.*

Lord, we pray to you, the Holy One who comes to us. Come to us with new beginnings. Come to us with healing for festering wounds. Come to us with light for our shadows. Come to us with peace for our conflicts, wholeness for our brokenness, hope for our despair, and power to overcome our doubts and fears. Come to us that we may come closer to each other and to those in need. Come to us in Jesus Christ and make us ready to let him live in us. *Amen.*

Eternal God, you are not limited by time and space, but we watch the passage of time, remembering our past and anticipating our future. In this Advent and Christmas season, help us to live watchfully, between the already and the not yet. Teach us to glory in your light which has come in Christ. Give us courage to allow your light to shine in us and through us. Reveal the fullness of your presence to us in this Advent season—and in all the seasons of our lives. *Amen.*

O Living Christ, you were, you are, you come! Clothe us with garments of celebration, that we may be prepared for the feast of your birth. Be born in us, we pray, that hope may sustain us, that vision may animate us, that love may reveal your presence within us. Sift from our lives all that distorts our nature and separates us from you and your love. Take what is righteous and good in us, and increase it as a blessing for others. Receive our prayers, and lead us on our journey of faith. In Christ's name. *Amen.*

O Holy One, you surround my life with grace, and I confess that I often do not see as I should. Your presence in my life takes me by surprise. I see only the outer signs: the baby, the feeding-place for the cattle, the tired mother and father. Sometimes I am unaware of your presence. Help me to know you, not just in the angel's song, but in the ordinary happenings of each day, that I may be a channel of your love and grace in Jesus Christ, in whose name I pray. *Amen.*

O God, lead us into the midst of this amazing world—hurting and desperate though it be. Challenge and unsettle us, even as you comfort and sustain us. Speak through us to those who may miss your coming: the pious who are trying too hard, the bitter who will not forgive, and the sick who are too weak to try. And when *we* are the pious, the bitter, and the sick, send someone to speak again to us your word of life. *Amen.*

O God of mangers, God of lullabies, simple shepherds, and silence, you knew exactly what we needed. Forgive us our clamors for what we want, while we miss what we really need. Turn on the Light again above the stable and let it shine into our confused hearts. Visit our busy lives with quiet grace. Still our hurrying, and give us moments when we see in the face of Jesus Christ how to want what we need. We long to be at Bethlehem where he is born in us, that we may become a crossroads where love is lived out in his name for the least and for the lost. *Amen.*

Loving Lord God, deliver us from fear and from the haste which fear causes, lest we shun the Light and Love by which we may be judged and healed. When at last—in the midst of the world's night—the Child is born, give us wisdom to kneel and joy to serve, that sharing in your glory we may be saved from doubt and pride. *Amen.*

Eternal God, we pray that you might give our words the power of deeds in a world which contains people who are desperate, grieving, sick, homeless, confused, lonely, and burned out. As we stop to help or kneel to serve, enable us to do and be what you call us to in the miracle of Bethlehem. *Amen.*

Gracious God, send angels singing good news for our times of gloom and discouragement, our times of failure and despair. Send us dreams to unsettle our complacency and to challenge our easy answers. Give us journeys to make when we are content with the status quo. Come with love for our estrangements, our loneliness, and our doubt. May Christ be born in us, that we may live like him and follow him in ministries of compassion and caring. In his name we pray. *Amen.*

God, we are as confounded as Joseph and Mary, as busy as the innkeepers, as lonely as the shepherds, as frightened as Herod, as wayfaring as the Magi. Turn us again to the place where, with quietness, you wrap up your truth and promise, your love and salvation in the Child born in a rude stable. We would ponder these things as the noise and clamor of the world is stilled for a time and there is a peace that settles deep within us. Bring us to Bethlehem, to the place where he was homeless but where we are truly at home. *Amen.*

Donald J. Shelby is Senior Minister of First United Methodist Church in Santa Monica, California. A graduate of Baker University in Kansas and of the School of Theology at Claremont, he has been pastor of St. Mark's United Methodist Church in San Diego and was founding pastor of St. Matthew's United Methodist Church in Hacienda Heights.

His hobbies include such diverse interests as gardening and bicycling. Mr. Shelby is active in community programs, having served in the past as Vice President of NCCJ (National Conference on Christians and Jews). He has led seminar tours to Wesley's England, the Holy Land, and the places of Paul's journeys through Turkey, Greece, and Italy.

As an author, Mr. Shelby has previously written three books for The Upper Room: *Meeting the Messiah*, *Bold Expectations of the Gospel*, and *Forever Beginning*.